Cute Amigurumi Monsters

Whether you choose one, two, or all 10 of these little monsters, you'll have big fun with them. Each playful figure is capable of standing on its own two feet.

LEISURE ARTS, INC. • Maumelle, Arkansas

Sunny
Pom-pom

SUNNY

●●○○ EASY

Finished Size:
Approximately 9" (23 cm) tall

SHOPPING LIST

Yarn (Medium Weight) 4

[7 ounces 364 yards
(198 grams, 333 meters) per skein]:
- ☐ Yellow - 1 skein
- ☐ White - 30 yards (27.5 meters)
- ☐ Brown - small amount
- ☐ Pink - small amount

[5 ounces, 236 yards
(141 grams, 215 meters) per skein]:
- ☐ Grey - 15 yards (13.5 meters)

Crochet Hooks
- ☐ Size E (3.5 mm) **and**
- ☐ Size G (4 mm)

Additional Supplies
- ☐ Yarn needle
- ☐ Polyester fiberfill

GAUGE INFORMATION

Gauge is not of great importance as long as your crochet fabric is dense ***(see Gauge, page 29)***.

STITCH GUIDE

SINGLE CROCHET 2 TOGETHER ***(abbreviated sc2tog)***
Pull up a loop in each of next 2 sc, YO and draw through all 3 loops on hook **(counts as one sc)**.

BODY

Rnd 1 (Right side)**:** With larger size hook and Yellow, make an adjustable loop to form a ring ***(Figs. 1a-d, page 30)***; work 6 sc in ring; do **not** join, place marker to indicate beginning of rnd ***(see Markers, page 29)***.

Rnd 2: 2 Sc in each sc around: 12 sc.

Rnd 3: Sc in each sc around.

Rnd 4: 2 Sc in each sc around: 24 sc.

Rnd 5: (Sc in next sc, 2 sc in next sc) around: 36 sc.

Rnds 6-17: Sc in each sc around; do **not** finish off.

FIRST LEG

Rnd 1: Sc in next 18 sc, leave remaining sc unworked; do **not** join, place marker to indicate beginning of rnd: 18 sc.

Rnd 2: Sc in each sc around.

Rnd 3: Sc in next 3 sc, 2 hdc in each of next 3 sc (toes), sc in each sc around; slip st in next sc, finish off: 21 sts.

SECOND LEG

Rnd 1: With **right** side facing, larger size hook, and leaving a long end for sewing, join Yellow with sc in first unworked sc on Rnd 17 of Body ***(see Joining With Sc, page 29)***; sc in each sc around; do **not** join, place marker to indicate beginning of rnd: 18 sc.

Rnd 2: Sc in each sc around.

Rnd 3: Sc in next 12 sc, 2 hdc in each of next 3 sc (toes), sc in next 3 sc; slip st in next sc, finish off: 21 sts.

Thread yarn needle with long end and sew opening between Legs closed.

Stuff Body and Legs firmly with polyester fiberfill.

SOLE (Make 2)

Rnd 1 (Right side)**:** With larger size hook and Yellow, make an adjustable loop to form a ring; ch 2 **(does not count as a st)**, work 12 hdc in ring; do **not** join, place marker to indicate beginning of rnd: 12 hdc.

Note: Loop a short piece of yarn around any stitch to mark Rnd 1 as **right** side.

Rnd 2: 2 Hdc in each hdc around; slip st in next hdc, finish off leaving a long end for sewing: 24 hdc.

With long ends, sew one Sole to bottom of each Leg.

HEAD

Rnd 1 (Right side)**:** With larger size hook and Yellow, make an adjustable loop to form a ring; work 6 sc in ring; do **not** join, place marker to indicate beginning of rnd.

Rnd 2: 2 Sc in each sc around: 12 sc.

Rnd 3: (2 Sc in next sc, sc in next sc) around: 18 sc.

Rnd 4: (2 Sc in next sc, sc in next 2 sc) around: 24 sc.

Rnd 5: (2 Sc in next sc, sc in next 3 sc) around: 30 sc.

Rnd 6: (2 Sc in next sc, sc in next 4 sc) around: 36 sc.

Rnds 7-11: Sc in each sc around.

Rnd 12: (Sc2tog, sc in next 4 sc) around: 30 sc.

Rnd 13: (Sc2tog, sc in next 3 sc) around: 24 sc.

Rnd 14: (Sc2tog, sc in next 2 sc) around: 18 sc.

Stuff Head firmly with polyester fiberfill.

Rnd 15: (Sc2tog, sc in next sc) around: 12 sc.

Rnd 16: Sc2tog around; slip st in next sc, finish off leaving a long end for sewing: 6 sc.

Thread yarn needle with long end. Weave needle through sts on Rnd 16 *(Fig. 5, page 30)* and pull **tightly** to close hole and secure end; do **not** cut yarn.

With same yarn and using photo on page 2 as a guide for placement, sew Head to Body.

ARM (Make 2)

Rnd 1 (Right side)**:** With larger size hook and Yellow, make an adjustable loop to form a ring; work 6 sc in ring; do **not** join, place marker to indicate beginning of rnd.

Note: Mark Rnd 1 as **right** side.

Rnd 2: 2 Sc in each sc around: 12 sc.

Rnds 3-7: Sc in each sc around.

Rnd 8: (Sc2tog, sc in next 2 sc) around: 9 sc.

Rnds 9-12: Sc in each sc around.

Slip st in next sc, finish off leaving a long end for sewing.

Stuff Arm lightly with polyester fiberfill.

Flatten Arms; using photo on page 2 as a guide for placement, sew Arms to sides of Body using long ends.

EYE

EYEBALL

Rnd 1 (Right side)**:** With smaller size hook and White, make an adjustable loop to form a ring; work 6 sc in ring; do **not** join, place marker to indicate beginning of rnd.

Rnd 2: 2 Sc in each sc around: 12 sc.

Rnd 3: (2 Sc in next sc, sc in next sc) around: 18 sc.

Rnd 4: (2 Sc in next sc, sc in next 2 sc) around: 24 sc.

Rnds 5-7: Sc in each sc around.

Rnd 8: (Sc2tog, sc in next 2 sc) around: 18 sc.

Stuff Eyeball firmly with polyester fiberfill.

Rnd 9: (Sc2tog, sc in next sc) around: 12 sc.

Rnd 10: Sc2tog around; slip st in next sc, finish off leaving a long end for sewing: 6 sc.

Thread yarn needle with long end. Weave needle through sts on Rnd 10 and pull **tightly** to close hole and secure end.

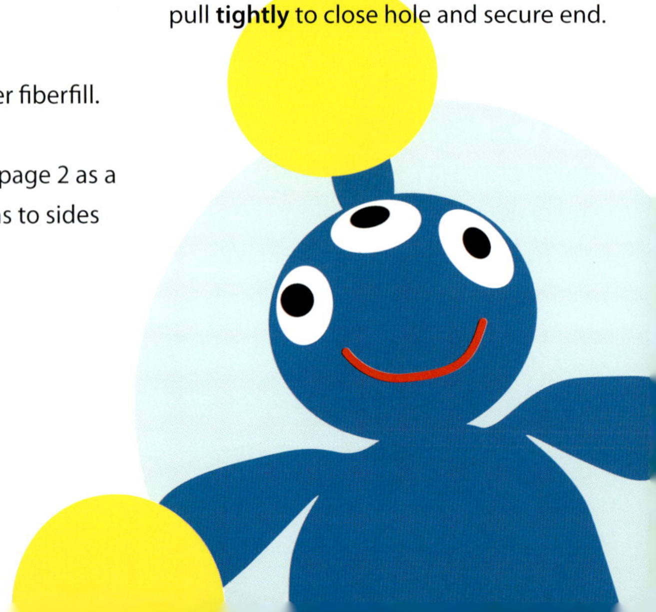

PUPIL

Rnd 1 (Right side)**:** With smaller size hook and Brown, make an adjustable loop to form a ring; work 6 sc in ring; do **not** join, place marker to indicate beginning of rnd.

Note: Mark Rnd 1 as **right** side.

Rnd 2: 2 Sc in each sc around; slip st in next sc, finish off leaving a long end for sewing: 12 sc.

EYE SOCKET

Rnd 1 (Right side)**:** With larger size hook and Yellow, make an adjustable loop to form a ring; work 6 sc in ring; do **not** join, place marker to indicate beginning of rnd.

Note: Mark Rnd 1 as **right** side.

Rnd 2: 2 Sc in each sc around: 12 sc.

Rnd 3: (2 Sc in next sc, sc in next sc) around: 18 sc.

Rnd 4: (2 Sc in next sc, sc in next 2 sc) around: 24 sc.

Rnd 5: Sc in each sc around.

Rnd 6: Sc in next 17 sc, hdc in next 7 sc (top); slip st in next sc, finish off leaving a long end for sewing.

Place Eyeball in Eye Socket with Rnd 1 of Eyeball at top of Eye Socket. Using long end, sew Eye Socket to Eyeball.

Using photo on page 2 as a guide for placement and long end, sew Pupil to Eyeball.

Using photo on page 2 as a guide for placement and Yellow, sew Eye to Head.

HORN (Make 2)

With larger size hook, Grey and leaving a long end for sewing, ch 12; being careful **not** to twist ch, join with slip st to form a ring.

Rnd 1 (Right side)**:** Ch 1, sc in same ch as joining and in each ch around; do **not** join, place marker to indicate beginning of rnd: 12 sc.

Note: Mark Rnd 1 as **right** side.

Rnd 2: Sc in each sc around.

Rnd 3: (Sc2tog, sc in next 2 sc) around: 9 sc.

Rnd 4: (Sc2tog, sc in next sc) around: 6 sc.

Rnd 5: Sc in each sc around.

Rnd 6: Sc2tog around; slip st in next sc, finish off leaving a long end for sewing: 3 sc.

Thread yarn needle with long end. Weave needle through sts on Rnd 6 and pull **tightly** to close hole and secure end.

Using photo on page 2 as a guide for placement and Grey, sew Horns to Head.

MOUTH

Using photo on page 2 as a guide for placement and outline stitch ***(Figs. 7a & b, page 30)***, add Pink mouth to Head.

POM-POM

●●○○ EASY

Finished Size:
Approximately 10" (25.5 cm) tall

SHOPPING LIST

Yarn (Medium Weight) MEDIUM 4
[7 ounces 364 yards
(198 grams, 333 meters) per skein]:

- ☐ Blue - 1 skein
- ☐ Yellow - 55 yards (51 meters)
- ☐ White - small amount
- ☐ Brown - small amount
- ☐ Red - small amount

Crochet Hooks

- ☐ Size E (3.5 mm) **and**
- ☐ Size G (4 mm)

Additional Supplies

- ☐ Yarn needle
- ☐ Polyester fiberfill

GAUGE INFORMATION

Gauge is not of great importance as long as your crochet fabric is dense *(see Gauge, page 29)*.

STITCH GUIDE

SINGLE CROCHET 2 TOGETHER *(abbreviated sc2tog)*
Pull up a loop in each of next 2 sc, YO and draw through all 3 loops on hook **(counts as one sc)**.

BODY

Rnd 1 (Right side)**:** With larger size hook and Blue, make an adjustable loop to form a ring ***(Figs. 1a-d, page 30)***; work 6 sc in ring; do **not** join, place marker to indicate beginning of rnd ***(see Markers, page 29)***.

Rnd 2: 2 Sc in each sc around: 12 sc.

Rnd 3: Sc in each sc around.

Rnd 4: 2 Sc in each sc around: 24 sc.

Rnd 5: (Sc in next sc, 2 sc in next sc) around: 36 sc.

Rnds 6-17: Sc in each sc around; do **not** finish off.

FIRST LEG

Rnd 1: Sc in next 18 sc, leave remaining sc unworked; do **not** join, place marker to indicate beginning of rnd: 18 sc.

Rnd 2: Sc in each sc around.

Rnd 3: Sc in next 3 sc, 2 hdc in each of next 3 sc (toes), sc in each sc around; slip st in next sc, finish off: 21 sts.

SECOND LEG

Rnd 1: With **right** side facing, larger size hook, and leaving a long end for sewing, join Blue with sc in first unworked sc on Rnd 17 of Body ***(see Joining With Sc, page 29)***; sc in each sc around; do **not** join, place marker to indicate beginning of rnd: 18 sc.

Rnd 2: Sc in each sc around.

Rnd 3: Sc in next 12 sc, 2 hdc in each of next 3 sc (toes), sc in next 3 sc; slip st in next sc, finish off: 21 sts.

Thread yarn needle with long end and sew opening between Legs closed.

Stuff Body and Legs firmly with polyester fiberfill.

SOLE (Make 2)

Rnd 1 (Right side)**:** With larger size hook and Blue, make an adjustable loop to form a ring; ch 2 **(does not count as a st)**, work 12 hdc in ring; do **not** join, place marker to indicate beginning of rnd: 12 hdc.

Note: Loop a short piece of yarn around any stitch to mark Rnd 1 as **right** side.

Rnd 2: 2 Hdc in each hdc around; slip st in next hdc, finish off leaving a long end for sewing: 24 hdc.

With long ends, sew one Sole to bottom of each Leg.

HEAD

Rnd 1 (Right side)**:** With larger size hook and Blue, make an adjustable loop to form a ring; work 6 sc in ring; do **not** join, place marker to indicate beginning of rnd.

Rnd 2: 2 Sc in each sc around: 12 sc.

Rnd 3: (2 Sc in next sc, sc in next sc) around: 18 sc.

Rnd 4: (2 Sc in next sc, sc in next 2 sc) around: 24 sc.

Rnd 5: (2 Sc in next sc, sc in next 3 sc) around: 30 sc.

Rnd 6: (2 Sc in next sc, sc in next 4 sc) around: 36 sc.

Rnds 7-11: Sc in each sc around.

Rnd 12: (Sc2tog, sc in next 4 sc) around: 30 sc.

Rnd 13: (Sc2tog, sc in next 3 sc) around: 24 sc.

Rnd 14: (Sc2tog, sc in next 2 sc) around: 18 sc.

Stuff Head firmly with polyester fiberfill.

Rnd 15: (Sc2tog, sc in next sc) around: 12 sc.

Rnd 16: Sc2tog around; slip st in next sc, finish off leaving a long end for sewing: 6 sc.

Thread yarn needle with long end. Weave needle through sts on Rnd 16 ***(Fig. 5, page 30)*** and pull **tightly** to close hole and secure end; do **not** cut yarn.

With same yarn and using photo on page 2 as a guide for placement, sew Head to Body.

ARM (Make 2)

Rnd 1 (Right side)**:** With larger size hook and Blue, make an adjustable loop to form a ring; work 6 sc in ring; do **not** join, place marker to indicate beginning of rnd.

Note: Mark Rnd 1 as **right** side.

Rnd 2: 2 Sc in each sc around: 12 sc.

Rnds 3-7: Sc in each sc around.

Rnd 8: (Sc2tog, sc in next 2 sc) around: 9 sc.

Rnds 9-12: Sc in each sc around.

Slip st in next sc, finish off leaving a long end for sewing.

Stuff Arm lightly with polyester fiberfill.

Flatten Arms; using photo on page 2 as a guide for placement, sew Arms to sides of Body using long ends.

EYE (Make 3)

Rnd 1 (Right side)**:** With smaller size hook and Brown, make an adjustable loop to form a ring; work 6 sc in ring, changing to White in last sc ***(Fig. 4, page 30)***; cut Brown; do **not** join, place marker to indicate beginning of rnd.

Note: Mark Rnd 1 as **right** side.

Rnd 2: 2 Sc in each sc around; slip st in next sc, finish off leaving a long end for sewing: 12 sc.

Using photo as a guide for placement, sew Eyes to Head.

STALK

With smaller size hook and Blue, ch 5.

Row 1 (Right side)**:** Sc in back ridge of second ch from hook and each ch across ***(Fig. 2, page 30)***: 4 sc.

Note: Mark Row 1 as **right** side.

Rows 2-5: Ch 1, turn; sc in each sc across.

Finish off leaving a long end for sewing.

Thread yarn needle with long end.

With **wrong** side together, whipstitch Row 5 to beginning ch to form a tube ***(Fig. 6, page 30)***; secure end, do **not** cut yarn.
With same yarn, sew Stalk to center top of Head.

Stuff Stalk firmly with polyester fiberfill.

POM-POM (Make 3)

Cut a piece of cardboard 3" (7.5 cm) square. Wind the Yellow around the cardboard approximately 100 times ***(Fig. A)***.
Carefully slip the yarn off the cardboard and firmly tie an 18" (45.5 cm) length of Yellow around the middle ***(Fig. B)***. Leave yarn ends long enough to attach the pom-pom. Cut the loops on both ends and trim the pom-pom into a smooth ball ***(Fig. C)***.

Fig. A

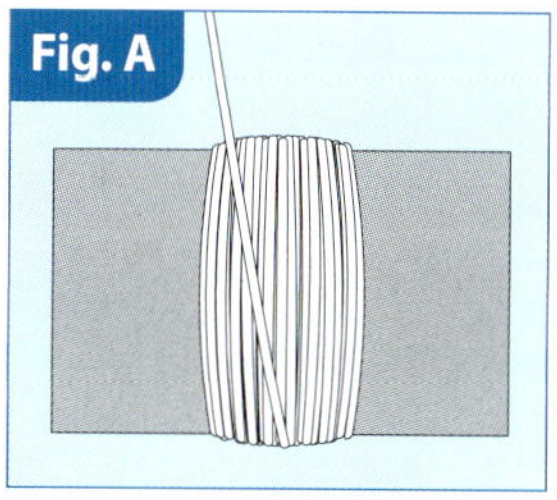

Fig. B

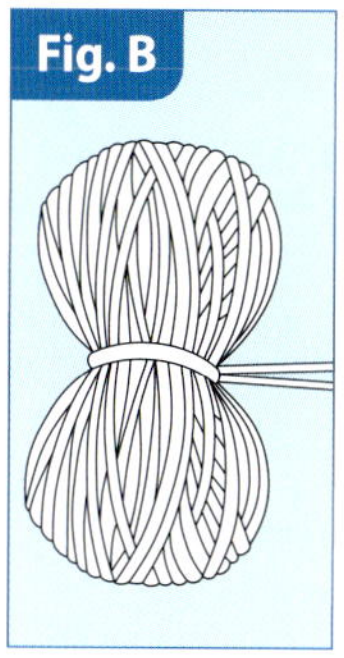

Fig. C

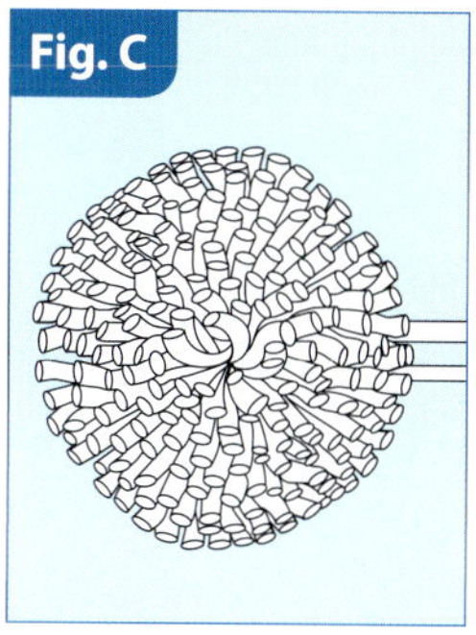

Attach one pom-pom to end of each Arm and one to top of Stalk.

MOUTH

Using photo on page 2 as a guide for placement and outline stitch ***(Figs. 7a & b, page 30)***, add Red mouth to Head.

Flame
Mohawk

MOHAWK

●●○○ EASY

Finished Size:
Approximately 7½" (19 cm) tall (excluding Mohawk)

SHOPPING LIST

Yarn (Medium Weight) MEDIUM 4

[7 ounces 364 yards (198 grams, 333 meters) per skein]:

- ☐ Green - 1 skein
- ☐ White - small amount
- ☐ Brown - small amount
- ☐ Red - small amount

Crochet Hooks

- ☐ Size E (3.5 mm) **and**
- ☐ Size G (4 mm)

Additional Supplies

- ☐ Yarn needle
- ☐ Polyester fiberfill

GAUGE INFORMATION

Gauge is not of great importance as long as your crochet fabric is dense *(see Gauge, page 29)*.

STITCH GUIDE

SINGLE CROCHET 2 TOGETHER *(abbreviated sc2tog)*
Pull up a loop in each of next 2 sc, YO and draw through all 3 loops on hook **(counts as one sc)**.

BODY

Rnd 1 (Right side)**:** With larger size hook and Green, make an adjustable loop to form a ring ***(Figs. 1a-d, page 30)***; work 6 sc in ring; do **not** join, place marker to indicate beginning of rnd ***(see Markers, page 29)***.

Rnd 2: 2 Sc in each sc around: 12 sc.

Rnd 3: Sc in each sc around.

Rnd 4: 2 Sc in each sc around: 24 sc.

Rnd 5: (Sc in next sc, 2 sc in next sc) around: 36 sc.

Rnds 6-17: Sc in each sc around; do **not** finish off.

FIRST LEG

Rnd 1: Sc in next 18 sc, leave remaining sc unworked; do **not** join, place marker to indicate beginning of rnd: 18 sc.

Rnd 2: Sc in each sc around.

Rnd 3: Sc in next 3 sc, 2 hdc in each of next 3 sc (toes), sc in each sc around; slip st in next sc, finish off: 21 sts.

SECOND LEG

Rnd 1: With **right** side facing, larger size hook, and leaving a long end for sewing, join Green with sc in first unworked sc on Rnd 17 of Body ***(see Joining With Sc, page 29)***; sc in each sc around; do **not** join, place marker to indicate beginning of rnd: 18 sc.

Rnd 2: Sc in each sc around.

Rnd 3: Sc in next 12 sc, 2 hdc in each of next 3 sc (toes), sc in next 3 sc; slip st in next sc, finish off: 21 sts.

Thread yarn needle with long end and sew opening between Legs closed.

Stuff Body and Legs firmly with polyester fiberfill.

SOLE (Make 2)

Rnd 1 (Right side)**:** With larger size hook and Green, make an adjustable loop to form a ring; ch 2 **(does not count as a st)**, work 12 hdc in ring; do **not** join, place marker to indicate beginning of rnd: 12 hdc.

Note: Loop a short piece of yarn around any stitch to mark Rnd 1 as **right** side.

Rnd 2: 2 Hdc in each hdc around; slip st in next hdc, finish off leaving a long end for sewing: 24 hdc.

With long ends, sew one Sole to bottom of each Leg.

HEAD

Rnd 1 (Right side)**:** With larger size hook and Green, make an adjustable loop to form a ring; work 6 sc in ring; do **not** join, place marker to indicate beginning of rnd.

Rnd 2: 2 Sc in each sc around: 12 sc.

Rnd 3: (2 Sc in next sc, sc in next sc) around: 18 sc.

Rnd 4: (2 Sc in next sc, sc in next 2 sc) around: 24 sc.

Rnd 5: (2 Sc in next sc, sc in next 3 sc) around: 30 sc.

Rnd 6: (2 Sc in next sc, sc in next 4 sc) around: 36 sc.

Rnds 7-11: Sc in each sc around.

Rnd 12: (Sc2tog, sc in next 4 sc) around: 30 sc.

Rnd 13: (Sc2tog, sc in next 3 sc) around: 24 sc.

Rnd 14: (Sc2tog, sc in next 2 sc) around: 18 sc.

Stuff Head firmly with polyester fiberfill.

Rnd 15: (Sc2tog, sc in next sc) around: 12 sc.

Rnd 16: Sc2tog around; slip st in next sc, finish off leaving a long end for sewing: 6 sc.

Thread yarn needle with long end. Weave needle through sts on Rnd 16 ***(Fig. 5, page 30)*** and pull **tightly** to close hole and secure end; do **not** cut yarn.

With same yarn and using photo on page 8 as a guide for placement, sew Head to Body.

ARM (Make 2)

Rnd 1 (Right side)**:** With larger size hook and Green, make an adjustable loop to form a ring; work 6 sc in ring; do **not** join, place marker to indicate beginning of rnd.

Note: Mark Rnd 1 as **right** side.

Rnd 2: 2 Sc in each sc around: 12 sc.

Rnds 3-7: Sc in each sc around.

Rnd 8: (Sc2tog, sc in next 2 sc) around: 9 sc.

Rnds 9-12: Sc in each sc around.

Slip st in next sc, finish off leaving a long end for sewing.

Stuff Arm lightly with polyester fiberfill.

Flatten Arms; using photo on page 8 as a guide for placement, sew Arms to sides of Body using long ends.

EYE (Make 3)

Rnd 1 (Right side)**:** With smaller size hook and Brown, make an adjustable loop to form a ring; work 6 sc in ring, changing to White in last sc ***(Fig. 4, page 30)***; cut Brown; do **not** join, place marker to indicate beginning of rnd.

Note: Mark Rnd 1 as **right** side.

Rnd 2: 2 Sc in each sc around; slip st in next sc, finish off leaving a long end for sewing: 12 sc.

Using photo as a guide for placement, sew Eyes to Head.

MOHAWK

Cut 18 strands of Green, each 4" (10 cm) long. Fold one strand in half. Using a crochet hook, draw the folded end up through a stitch on the top of the Head and pull the loose ends through the folded end ***(Fig. A)***; draw the knot up tightly. Add remaining strands across top of Head.

Fig. A

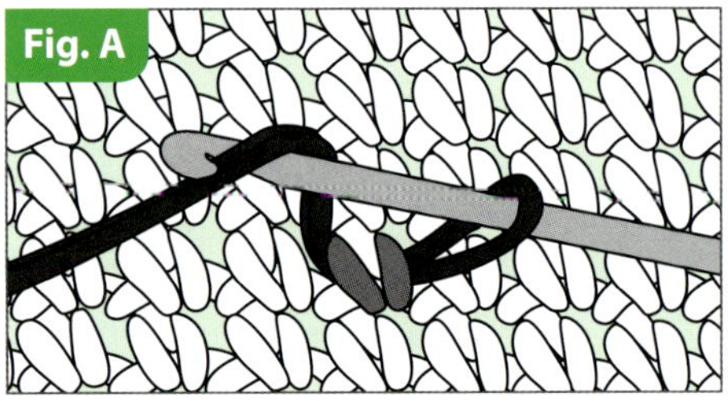

MOUTH

Using photo on page 8 as a guide for placement and outline stitch ***(Figs. 7a & b, page 30)***, add Red mouth to Head.

FLAME

●●○○ EASY

Finished Size:
Approximately 9½" (24 cm) tall

SHOPPING LIST

Yarn (Medium Weight) MEDIUM 4
[7 ounces 364 yards
(198 grams, 333 meters) per skein]:
- ☐ Orange - 1 skein
- ☐ White - 30 yards (27.5 meters)
- ☐ Brown - small amount
- ☐ Red - small amount

Crochet Hooks
- ☐ Size E (3.5 mm) **and**
- ☐ Size G (4 mm)

Additional Supplies
- ☐ Yarn needle
- ☐ Polyester fiberfill

GAUGE INFORMATION

Gauge is not of great importance as long as your crochet fabric is dense *(see Gauge, page 29)*.

STITCH GUIDE

SINGLE CROCHET 2 TOGETHER
(abbreviated sc2tog)
Pull up a loop in each of next 2 sc, YO and draw through all 3 loops on hook **(counts as one sc)**.

BODY

Rnd 1 (Right side)**:** With larger size hook and Orange, make an adjustable loop to form a ring ***(Figs. 1a-d, page 30)***; work 6 sc in ring; do **not** join, place marker to indicate beginning of rnd ***(see Markers, page 29)***.

Rnd 2: 2 Sc in each sc around: 12 sc.

Rnd 3: Sc in each sc around.

Rnd 4: 2 Sc in each sc around: 24 sc.

Rnd 5: (Sc in next sc, 2 sc in next sc) around: 36 sc.

Rnds 6-17: Sc in each sc around; do **not** finish off.

FIRST LEG

Rnd 1: Sc in next 18 sc, leave remaining sc unworked; do **not** join, place marker to indicate beginning of rnd: 18 sc.

Rnd 2: Sc in each sc around.

Rnd 3: Sc in next 3 sc, 2 hdc in each of next 3 sc (toes), sc in each sc around; slip st in next sc, finish off: 21 sts.

SECOND LEG

Rnd 1: With **right** side facing, larger size hook, and leaving a long end for sewing, join Orange with sc in first unworked sc on Rnd 17 of Body ***(see Joining With Sc, page 29)***; sc in each sc around; do **not** join, place marker to indicate beginning of rnd: 18 sc.

Rnd 2: Sc in each sc around.

Rnd 3: Sc in next 12 sc, 2 hdc in each of next 3 sc (toes), sc in next 3 sc; slip st in next sc, finish off: 21 sts.

Thread yarn needle with long end and sew opening between Legs closed.

Stuff Body and Legs firmly with polyester fiberfill.

SOLE (Make 2)

Rnd 1 (Right side)**:** With larger size hook and Orange, make an adjustable loop to form a ring; ch 2 **(does not count as a st)**, work 12 hdc in ring; do **not** join, place marker to indicate beginning of rnd: 12 hdc.

Note: Loop a short piece of yarn around any stitch to mark Rnd 1 as **right** side.

Rnd 2: 2 Hdc in each hdc around; slip st in next hdc, finish off leaving a long end for sewing: 24 hdc.

With long ends, sew one Sole to bottom of each Leg.

HEAD

Rnd 1 (Right side)**:** With larger size hook and Orange, make an adjustable loop to form a ring; work 6 sc in ring; do **not** join, place marker to indicate beginning of rnd.

Rnd 2: 2 Sc in each sc around: 12 sc.

Rnd 3: (2 Sc in next sc, sc in next sc) around: 18 sc.

Rnd 4: (2 Sc in next sc, sc in next 2 sc) around: 24 sc.

Rnd 5: (2 Sc in next sc, sc in next 3 sc) around: 30 sc.

Rnd 6: (2 Sc in next sc, sc in next 4 sc) around: 36 sc.

Rnds 7-11: Sc in each sc around.

Rnd 12: (Sc2tog, sc in next 4 sc) around: 30 sc.

Rnd 13: (Sc2tog, sc in next 3 sc) around: 24 sc.

Rnd 14: (Sc2tog, sc in next 2 sc) around: 18 sc.

Stuff Head firmly with polyester fiberfill.

Rnd 15: (Sc2tog, sc in next sc) around: 12 sc.

Rnd 16: Sc2tog around; slip st in next sc, finish off leaving a long end for sewing: 6 sc.

Thread yarn needle with long end. Weave needle through sts on Rnd 16 ***(Fig. 5, page 30)*** and pull **tightly** to close hole and secure end; do **not** cut yarn.

With same yarn and using photo on page 8 as a guide for placement, sew Head to Body.

ARM (Make 2)

Rnd 1 (Right side)**:** With larger size hook and Orange, make an adjustable loop to form a ring; work 6 sc in ring; do **not** join, place marker to indicate beginning of rnd.

Note: Mark Rnd 1 as **right** side.

Rnd 2: 2 Sc in each sc around: 12 sc.

Rnds 3-7: Sc in each sc around.

Rnd 8: (Sc2tog, sc in next 2 sc) around: 9 sc.

Rnds 9-12: Sc in each sc around.

Slip st in next sc, finish off leaving a long end for sewing.

Stuff Arm lightly with polyester fiberfill.

Flatten Arms; using photo on page 8 as a guide for placement, sew Arms to sides of Body using long ends.

EYE (Make 3)

EYEBALL

Rnd 1 (Right side)**:** With smaller size hook and Brown, make an adjustable loop to form a ring; work 6 sc in ring; do **not** join, place marker to indicate beginning of rnd.

Rnd 2: 2 Sc in each sc around, changing to White in last sc ***(Fig. 4, page 30)***; cut Brown: 12 sc.

Rnd 3: (2 Sc in next sc, sc in next sc) around: 18 sc.

Rnd 4: (2 Sc in next sc, sc in next 2 sc) around: 24 sc.

Rnds 5-7: Sc in each sc around.

Rnd 8: (Sc2tog, sc in next 2 sc) around: 18 sc.

Stuff Eyeball firmly with polyester fiberfill.

Rnd 9: (Sc2tog, sc in next sc) around: 12 sc.

Rnd 10: Sc2tog around; slip st in next sc, finish off leaving a long end for sewing: 6 sc.

Thread yarn needle with long end. Weave needle through sts on Rnd 10 and pull **tightly** to close hole and secure end.

STALK

With smaller size hook and Orange, ch 5.

Row 1 (Right side)**:** Sc in back ridge of second ch from hook and each ch across ***(Fig. 2, page 30)***: 4 sc.

Note: Mark Row 1 as **right** side.

Rows 2-5: Ch 1, turn; sc in each sc across.

Finish off leaving a long end for sewing.

Thread yarn needle with long end.

With **wrong** side together, whipstitch Row 5 to beginning ch to form a tube ***(Fig. 6, page 30)***; secure end, do **not** cut yarn.
With same yarn, sew Stalk to Rnd 10 of Eyeball.

Stuff Stalk firmly with polyester fiberfill.

Using photo on page 8 as a guide for placement and Orange, sew Stalks to Head.

MOUTH

Using photo on page 8 as a guide for placement and outline stitch ***(Figs. 7a & b, page 30)***, add Red mouth to Head.

Floppy
Shockster

FLOPPY

●●○○ EASY

Finished Size:
Approximately 9" (23 cm) tall

SHOPPING LIST

Yarn (Medium Weight) MEDIUM 4
[7 ounces 364 yards
(198 grams, 333 meters) per skein]:
- ☐ Blue - 1 skein
- ☐ White - 20 yards (18.5 meters)
- ☐ Red - small amount

Crochet Hooks
- ☐ Size E (3.5 mm) **and**
- ☐ Size G (4 mm)

Additional Supplies
- ☐ Yarn needle
- ☐ Polyester fiberfill

GAUGE INFORMATION

Gauge is not of great importance as long as your crochet fabric is dense *(see Gauge, page 29)*.

STITCH GUIDE

SINGLE CROCHET 2 TOGETHER *(abbreviated sc2tog)*
Pull up a loop in each of next 2 sc, YO and draw through all 3 loops on hook **(counts as one sc)**.

SINGLE CROCHET 3 TOGETHER *(abbreviated sc3tog)*
Pull up a loop in each of next 3 sc, YO and draw through all 4 loops on hook **(counts as one sc)**.

BODY

Rnd 1 (Right side)**:** With larger size hook and Blue, make an adjustable loop to form a ring ***(Figs. 1a-d, page 30)***; work 6 sc in ring; do **not** join, place marker to indicate beginning of rnd ***(see Markers, page 29)***.

Rnd 2: 2 Sc in each sc around: 12 sc.

Rnd 3: Sc in each sc around.

Rnd 4: 2 Sc in each sc around: 24 sc.

Rnd 5: (Sc in next sc, 2 sc in next sc) around: 36 sc.

Rnds 6-17: Sc in each sc around; do **not** finish off.

FIRST LEG

Rnd 1: Sc in next 18 sc, leave remaining sc unworked; do **not** join, place marker to indicate beginning of rnd: 18 sc.

Rnd 2: Sc in each sc around.

Rnd 3: Sc in next 3 sc, 2 hdc in each of next 3 sc (toes), sc in each sc around; slip st in next sc, finish off: 21 sts.

SECOND LEG

Rnd 1: With **right** side facing, larger size hook, and leaving a long end for sewing, join Blue with sc in first unworked sc on Rnd 17 of Body ***(see Joining With Sc, page 29)***; sc in each sc around; do **not** join, place marker to indicate beginning of rnd: 18 sc.

Rnd 2: Sc in each sc around.

Rnd 3: Sc in next 12 sc, 2 hdc in each of next 3 sc (toes), sc in next 3 sc; slip st in next sc, finish off: 21 sts.

Thread yarn needle with long end and sew opening between Legs closed.

Stuff Body and Legs firmly with polyester fiberfill.

SOLE (Make 2)

Rnd 1 (Right side)**:** With larger size hook and Blue, make an adjustable loop to form a ring; ch 2 **(does not count as a st)**, work 12 hdc in ring; do **not** join, place marker to indicate beginning of rnd: 12 hdc.

Note: Loop a short piece of yarn around any stitch to mark Rnd 1 as **right** side.

Rnd 2: 2 Hdc in each hdc around; slip st in next hdc, finish off leaving a long end for sewing: 24 hdc.

With long ends, sew one Sole to bottom of each Leg.

HEAD

Rnd 1 (Right side)**:** With larger size hook and Blue, make an adjustable loop to form a ring; work 6 sc in ring; do **not** join, place marker to indicate beginning of rnd.

Rnd 2: 2 Sc in each sc around: 12 sc.

Rnd 3: (2 Sc in next sc, sc in next sc) around: 18 sc.

Rnd 4: (2 Sc in next sc, sc in next 2 sc) around: 24 sc.

Rnd 5: (2 Sc in next sc, sc in next 3 sc) around: 30 sc.

Rnd 6: (2 Sc in next sc, sc in next 4 sc) around: 36 sc.

Rnds 7-11: Sc in each sc around.

Rnd 12: (Sc2tog, sc in next 4 sc) around: 30 sc.

Rnd 13: (Sc2tog, sc in next 3 sc) around: 24 sc.

Rnd 14: (Sc2tog, sc in next 2 sc) around: 18 sc.

Stuff Head firmly with polyester fiberfill.

Rnd 15: (Sc2tog, sc in next sc) around: 12 sc.

Rnd 16: Sc2tog around; slip st in next sc, finish off leaving a long end for sewing: 6 sc.

Thread yarn needle with long end. Weave needle through sts on Rnd 16 ***(Fig. 5, page 30)*** and pull **tightly** to close hole and secure end; do **not** cut yarn.

With same yarn and using photo on page 14 as a guide for placement, sew Head to Body.

ARM (Make 2)

Rnd 1 (Right side)**:** With larger size hook and Blue, make an adjustable loop to form a ring; work 6 sc in ring; do **not** join, place marker to indicate beginning of rnd.

Note: Mark Rnd 1 as **right** side.

Rnd 2: 2 Sc in each sc around: 12 sc.

Rnds 3-7: Sc in each sc around.

Rnd 8: (Sc2tog, sc in next 2 sc) around: 9 sc.

Rnds 9-12: Sc in each sc around.

Slip st in next sc, finish off leaving a long end for sewing.

Stuff Arm lightly with polyester fiberfill.

Flatten Arms; using photo on page 14 as a guide for placement, sew Arms to sides of Body using long ends.

EYEBALL (Make 2)

Rnd 1 (Right side)**:** With smaller size hook and Blue, make an adjustable loop to form a ring; work 6 sc in ring; do **not** join, place marker to indicate beginning of rnd.

Rnd 2: 2 Sc in each sc around, changing to White in last sc ***(Fig. 4, page 30)***; cut Blue: 12 sc.

Rnd 3: Sc in each sc around.

Rnd 4: (2 Sc in next sc, sc in next sc) around: 18 sc.

Rnd 5: Sc in each sc around.

Stuff Eye firmly with polyester fiberfill.

Rnd 6: (Sc2tog, sc in next sc) around: 12 sc.

Rnd 7: Sc2tog around; slip st in next sc, finish off leaving a long end for sewing: 6 sc.

Thread yarn needle with long end. Weave needle through sts on Rnd 7 and pull **tightly** to close hole and secure end.

Using photo on page 14 as a guide for placement and White, sew Eyeballs to Head.

EAR (Make 2)

With smaller size hook, Blue, and leaving a long end for sewing, ch 10.

Row 1 (Right side)**:** Sc in second ch from hook and in each ch across: 9 sc.

Note: Mark Row 1 as **right** side.

Row 2: Ch 1, turn; sc in each sc across.

Rows 3 and 4: Ch 1, turn; beginning in first sc, sc2tog, sc in each sc across to last 2 sc, sc2tog: 5 sc.

Row 5: Ch 1, turn; beginning in first sc, sc2tog, sc in next sc, sc2tog: 3 sc.

Row 6: Ch 1, turn; sc3tog; finish off.

Thread yarn needle with long end. Cupping Row 1 of Ear, sew to Head using photo on page 14 as a guide for placement.

MOUTH

Using photo on page 14 as a guide for placement and outline stitch ***(Figs. 7a & b, page 30)***, add Red mouth to Head.

SHOCKSTER

●●○○ EASY

Finished Size:
Approximately 7½" (19 cm) tall

SHOPPING LIST

Yarn (Medium Weight) MEDIUM 4
[7 ounces 364 yards
(198 grams, 333 meters) per skein]:
- ☐ Pink - 1 skein
- ☐ White - 15 yards (13.5 meters)
- ☐ Brown - small amount
- ☐ Red - small amount

Crochet Hooks
- ☐ Size E (3.5 mm) **and**
- ☐ Size G (4 mm)

Additional Supplies
- ☐ Yarn needle
- ☐ Polyester fiberfill

GAUGE INFORMATION

Gauge is not of great importance as long as your crochet fabric is dense ***(see Gauge, page 29)***.

STITCH GUIDE

SINGLE CROCHET 2 TOGETHER
(abbreviated sc2tog)
Pull up a loop in each of next 2 sc, YO and draw through all 3 loops on hook **(counts as one sc)**.

BODY

Rnd 1 (Right side)**:** With larger size hook and Pink, make an adjustable loop to form a ring ***(Figs. 1a-d, page 30)***; work 6 sc in ring; do **not** join, place marker to indicate beginning of rnd ***(see Markers, page 29)***.

Rnd 2: 2 Sc in each sc around: 12 sc.

Rnd 3: Sc in each sc around.

Rnd 4: 2 Sc in each sc around: 24 sc.

Rnd 5: (Sc in next sc, 2 sc in next sc) around: 36 sc.

Rnds 6-17: Sc in each sc around; do **not** finish off.

FIRST LEG

Rnd 1: Sc in next 18 sc, leave remaining sc unworked; do **not** join, place marker to indicate beginning of rnd: 18 sc.

Rnd 2: Sc in each sc around.

Rnd 3: Sc in next 3 sc, 2 hdc in each of next 3 sc (toes), sc in each sc around; slip st in next sc, finish off: 21 sts.

SECOND LEG

Rnd 1: With **right** side facing, larger size hook, and leaving a long end for sewing, join Pink with sc in first unworked sc on Rnd 17 of Body ***(see Joining With Sc, page 29)***; sc in each sc around; do **not** join, place marker to indicate beginning of rnd: 18 sc.

Rnd 2: Sc in each sc around.

Rnd 3: Sc in next 12 sc, 2 hdc in each of next 3 sc (toes), sc in next 3 sc; slip st in next sc, finish off: 21 sts.

Thread yarn needle with long end and sew opening between Legs closed.

Stuff Body and Legs firmly with polyester fiberfill.

SOLE (Make 2)

Rnd 1 (Right side)**:** With larger size hook and Pink, make an adjustable loop to form a ring; ch 2 **(does not count as a st)**, work 12 hdc in ring; do **not** join, place marker to indicate beginning of rnd: 12 hdc.

Note: Loop a short piece of yarn around any stitch to mark Rnd 1 as **right** side.

Rnd 2: 2 Hdc in each hdc around; slip st in next hdc, finish off leaving a long end for sewing: 24 hdc.

With long ends, sew one Sole to bottom of each Leg.

HEAD

Rnd 1 (Right side)**:** With larger size hook and Pink, make an adjustable loop to form a ring; work 6 sc in ring; do **not** join, place marker to indicate beginning of rnd.

Rnd 2: 2 Sc in each sc around: 12 sc.

Rnd 3: (2 Sc in next sc, sc in next sc) around: 18 sc.

Rnd 4: (2 Sc in next sc, sc in next 2 sc) around: 24 sc.

Rnd 5: (2 Sc in next sc, sc in next 3 sc) around: 30 sc.

Rnd 6: (2 Sc in next sc, sc in next 4 sc) around: 36 sc.

Rnds 7-11: Sc in each sc around.

Rnd 12: (Sc2tog, sc in next 4 sc) around: 30 sc.

Rnd 13: (Sc2tog, sc in next 3 sc) around: 24 sc.

Rnd 14: (Sc2tog, sc in next 2 sc) around: 18 sc.

Stuff Head firmly with polyester fiberfill.

Rnd 15: (Sc2tog, sc in next sc) around: 12 sc.

Rnd 16: Sc2tog around; slip st in next sc, finish off leaving a long end for sewing: 6 sc.

Thread yarn needle with long end. Weave needle through sts on Rnd 16 ***(Fig. 5, page 30)*** and pull **tightly** to close hole and secure end; do **not** cut yarn.

With same yarn and using photo on page 14 as a guide for placement, sew Head to Body.

ARM (Make 2)

Rnd 1 (Right side)**:** With larger size hook and Pink, make an adjustable loop to form a ring; work 6 sc in ring; do **not** join, place marker to indicate beginning of rnd.

Note: Mark Rnd 1 as **right** side.

Rnd 2: 2 Sc in each sc around: 12 sc.

Rnds 3-7: Sc in each sc around.

Rnd 8: (Sc2tog, sc in next 2 sc) around: 9 sc.

Rnds 9-12: Sc in each sc around.

Slip st in next sc, finish off leaving a long end for sewing.

Stuff Arm lightly with polyester fiberfill.

Flatten Arms; using photo on page 14 as a guide for placement, sew Arms to sides of Body using long ends.

EYE (Make 2)

Rnd 1 (Right side)**:** With smaller size hook and Brown, make an adjustable loop to form a ring; work 6 sc in ring; do **not** join, place marker to indicate beginning of rnd.

Rnd 2: 2 Sc in each sc around, changing to White in last sc ***(Fig. 4, page 30)***; cut Brown: 12 sc.

Rnd 3: (2 Sc in next sc, sc in next sc) around: 18 sc.

Rnd 4: (2 Sc in next sc, sc in next 2 sc) around, changing to Pink in last sc: 24 sc.

Rnds 5-7: Sc in each sc around.

Rnd 8: (Sc2tog, sc in next 2 sc) around: 18 sc.

Stuff Eye firmly with polyester fiberfill.

Rnd 9: (Sc2tog, sc in next sc) around: 12 sc.

Rnd 10: Sc2tog around; slip st in next sc, finish off leaving a long end for sewing: 6 sc.

Thread yarn needle with long end. Weave needle through sts on Rnd 10 and pull **tightly** to close hole and secure end.

Using photo on page 14 as a guide for placement and Pink, sew Eyes to Head.

MOUTH

Using photo on page 14 as a guide for placement and outline stitch ***(Figs. 7a & b, page 30)***, add Red mouth to Head.

SINGLETON

Shown on page 20.

●●○○ **EASY**

Finished Size:
Approximately 8½" (21.5 cm) tall

SHOPPING LIST

Yarn (Medium Weight) MEDIUM 4

[7 ounces 364 yards
(198 grams, 333 meters) per skein]:
- ☐ Purple - 1 skein
- ☐ White - 10 yards (9 meters)
- ☐ Blue - small amount
- ☐ Red - small amount

[5 ounces 236 yards
(141 grams, 215 meters) per skein]:
- ☐ Grey - 15 yards (13.5 meters)

Crochet Hooks
- ☐ Size E (3.5 mm) **and**
- ☐ Size G (4 mm)

Additional Supplies
- ☐ Yarn needle
- ☐ Polyester fiberfill

GAUGE INFORMATION

Gauge is not of great importance as long as your crochet fabric is dense *(see Gauge, page 29)*.

STITCH GUIDE

SINGLE CROCHET 2 TOGETHER
(abbreviated sc2tog)
Pull up a loop in each of next 2 sc, YO and draw through all 3 loops on hook **(counts as one sc)**.

BODY

Rnd 1 (Right side)**:** With larger size hook and Purple, make an adjustable loop to form a ring ***(Figs. 1a-d, page 30)***; work 6 sc in ring; do **not** join, place marker to indicate beginning of rnd ***(see Markers, page 29)***.

Rnd 2: 2 Sc in each sc around: 12 sc.

Rnd 3: Sc in each sc around.

Rnd 4: 2 Sc in each sc around: 24 sc.

Rnd 5: (Sc in next sc, 2 sc in next sc) around: 36 sc.

Rnds 6-17: Sc in each sc around; do **not** finish off.

FIRST LEG

Rnd 1: Sc in next 18 sc, leave remaining sc unworked; do **not** join, place marker to indicate beginning of rnd: 18 sc.

Rnd 2: Sc in each sc around.

Rnd 3: Sc in next 3 sc, 2 hdc in each of next 3 sc (toes), sc in each sc around; slip st in next sc, finish off: 21 sts.

SECOND LEG

Rnd 1: With **right** side facing, larger size hook, and leaving a long end for sewing, join Purple with sc in first unworked sc on Rnd 17 of Body ***(see Joining With Sc, page 29)***; sc in each sc around; do **not** join, place marker to indicate beginning of rnd: 18 sc.

Rnd 2: Sc in each sc around.

Rnd 3: Sc in next 12 sc, 2 hdc in each of next 3 sc (toes), sc in next 3 sc; slip st in next sc, finish off: 21 sts.

Thread yarn needle with long end and sew opening between Legs closed.

Stuff Body and Legs firmly with polyester fiberfill.

SOLE (Make 2)

Rnd 1 (Right side)**:** With larger size hook and Purple, make an adjustable loop to form a ring; ch 2 **(does not count as a st)**, work 12 hdc in ring; do **not** join, place marker to indicate beginning of rnd: 12 hdc.

Note: Mark Row 1 as **right** side.

Rnd 2: 2 Hdc in each hdc around; slip st in next hdc, finish off leaving a long end for sewing: 24 hdc.

With long ends, sew one Sole to bottom of each Leg.

HEAD

Rnd 1 (Right side)**:** With larger size hook and Purple, make an adjustable loop to form a ring; work 6 sc in ring; do **not** join, place marker to indicate beginning of rnd.

Rnd 2: 2 Sc in each sc around: 12 sc.

Rnd 3: (2 Sc in next sc, sc in next sc) around: 18 sc.

Singleton
Pinky

Rnd 4: (2 Sc in next sc, sc in next 2 sc) around: 24 sc.

Rnd 5: (2 Sc in next sc, sc in next 3 sc) around: 30 sc.

Rnd 6: (2 Sc in next sc, sc in next 4 sc) around: 36 sc.

Rnds 7-11: Sc in each sc around.

Rnd 12: (Sc2tog, sc in next 4 sc) around: 30 sc.

Rnd 13: (Sc2tog, sc in next 3 sc) around: 24 sc.

Rnd 14: (Sc2tog, sc in next 2 sc) around: 18 sc.

Stuff Head firmly with polyester fiberfill.

Rnd 15: (Sc2tog, sc in next sc) around: 12 sc.

Rnd 16: Sc2tog around; slip st in next sc, finish off leaving a long end for sewing: 6 sc.

Thread yarn needle with long end. Weave needle through sts on Rnd 16 ***(Fig. 5, page 30)*** and pull **tightly** to close hole and secure end; do **not** cut yarn.

With same yarn and using photo as a guide for placement, sew Head to Body.

ARM (Make 2)

Rnd 1 (Right side)**:** With larger size hook and Purple, make an adjustable loop to form a ring; work 6 sc in ring; do **not** join, place marker to indicate beginning of rnd.

Note: Mark Rnd 1 as **right** side.

Rnd 2: 2 Sc in each sc around: 12 sc.

Rnds 3-7: Sc in each sc around.

Rnd 8: (Sc2tog, sc in next 2 sc) around: 9 sc.

Rnds 9-12: Sc in each sc around.

Slip st in next sc, finish off leaving a long end for sewing.

Stuff Arm lightly with polyester fiberfill.

Flatten Arms; using photo as a guide for placement, sew Arms to sides of Body using long ends.

EYE

Rnd 1 (Right side)**:** With smaller size hook and Blue, make an adjustable loop to form a ring; work 6 sc in ring, changing to White in last sc ***(Fig. 4, page 30)***; cut Blue; do **not** join, place marker to indicate beginning of rnd.

Note: Mark Rnd 1 as **right** side.

Rnd 2: 2 Sc in each sc around: 12 sc.

Rnd 3: (2 Sc in next sc, sc in next sc) around; slip st in next sc, finish off leaving a long end for sewing: 18 sc.

Using photo as a guide for placement and long end, sew Eye to Head.

HORN

Rnd 1 (Right side)**:** With larger size hook and Grey, make an adjustable loop to form a ring; work 4 sc in ring; do **not** join, place marker to indicate beginning of rnd.

Rnd 2: 2 Sc in each sc around: 8 sc.

Rnd 3: 2 Sc in next sc, sc in each sc around: 9 sc.

Rnds 4-7: Sc in each sc around.

Slip st in next sc, finish off leaving a long end for sewing.

Stuff Horn firmly with polyester fiberfill.

Using photo as a guide for placement and Grey, sew Horn to Head.

MOUTH

Using photo as a guide for placement and outline stitch ***(Figs. 7a & b, page 30)***, add Red mouth to Head.

PINKY

●●○○ EASY

Finished Size:
Approximately 7½" (19 cm) tall (excluding Eyes)

SHOPPING LIST

Yarn (Medium Weight) MEDIUM 4
[7 ounces 364 yards
(198 grams, 333 meters) per skein]:
- ☐ Pink - 1 skein
- ☐ White - 30 yards (27.5 meters)
- ☐ Brown - small amount
- ☐ Red - small amount

Crochet Hooks
- ☐ Size E (3.5 mm) **and**
- ☐ Size G (4 mm)

Additional Supplies
- ☐ Yarn needle
- ☐ Polyester fiberfill

GAUGE INFORMATION

Gauge is not of great importance as long as your crochet fabric is dense *(see Gauge, page 29)*.

STITCH GUIDE

SINGLE CROCHET 2 TOGETHER ***(abbreviated sc2tog)***
Pull up a loop in each of next 2 sc, YO and draw through all 3 loops on hook **(counts as one sc)**.

BODY

Rnd 1 (Right side)**:** With larger size hook and Pink, make an adjustable loop to form a ring ***(Figs. 1a-d, page 30)***; work 6 sc in ring; do **not** join, place marker to indicate beginning of rnd ***(see Markers, page 29)***.

Rnd 2: 2 Sc in each sc around: 12 sc.

Rnd 3: Sc in each sc around.

Rnd 4: 2 Sc in each sc around: 24 sc.

Rnd 5: (Sc in next sc, 2 sc in next sc) around: 36 sc.

Rnds 6-17: Sc in each sc around; do **not** finish off.

FIRST LEG

Rnd 1: Sc in next 18 sc, leave remaining sc unworked; do **not** join, place marker to indicate beginning of rnd: 18 sc.

Rnd 2: Sc in each sc around.

Rnd 3: Sc in next 3 sc, 2 hdc in each of next 3 sc (toes), sc in each sc around; slip st in next sc, finish off: 21 sts.

SECOND LEG

Rnd 1: With **right** side facing, larger size hook, and leaving a long end for sewing, join Pink with sc in first unworked sc on Rnd 17 of Body ***(see Joining With Sc, page 29)***; sc in each sc around; do **not** join, place marker to indicate beginning of rnd: 18 sc.

Rnd 2: Sc in each sc around.

Rnd 3: Sc in next 12 sc, 2 hdc in each of next 3 sc (toes), sc in next 3 sc; slip st in next sc, finish off: 21 sts.

Thread yarn needle with long end and sew opening between Legs closed.

Stuff Body and Legs firmly with polyester fiberfill.

SOLE (Make 2)

Rnd 1 (Right side)**:** With larger size hook and Pink, make an adjustable loop to form a ring; ch 2 **(does not count as a st)**, work 12 hdc in ring; do **not** join, place marker to indicate beginning of rnd: 12 hdc.

Note: Loop a short piece of yarn around any stitch to mark Rnd 1 as **right** side.

Rnd 2: 2 Hdc in each hdc around; slip st in next hdc, finish off leaving a long end for sewing: 24 hdc.

With long ends, sew one Sole to bottom of each Leg.

HEAD

Rnd 1 (Right side)**:** With larger size hook and Pink, make an adjustable loop to form a ring; work 6 sc in ring; do **not** join, place marker to indicate beginning of rnd.

Rnd 2: 2 Sc in each sc around: 12 sc.

Rnd 3: (2 Sc in next sc, sc in next sc) around: 18 sc.

Rnd 4: (2 Sc in next sc, sc in next 2 sc) around: 24 sc.

Rnd 5: (2 Sc in next sc, sc in next 3 sc) around: 30 sc.

Rnd 6: (2 Sc in next sc, sc in next 4 sc) around: 36 sc.

Rnds 7-11: Sc in each sc around.

Rnd 12: (Sc2tog, sc in next 4 sc) around: 30 sc.

Rnd 13: (Sc2tog, sc in next 3 sc) around: 24 sc.

Rnd 14: (Sc2tog, sc in next 2 sc) around: 18 sc.

Stuff Head firmly with polyester fiberfill.

Rnd 15: (Sc2tog, sc in next sc) around: 12 sc.

Rnd 16: Sc2tog around; slip st in next sc, finish off leaving a long end for sewing: 6 sc.

Thread yarn needle with long end. Weave needle through sts on Rnd 16 ***(Fig. 5, page 30)*** and pull **tightly** to close hole and secure end; do **not** cut yarn.

With same yarn and using photo on page 20 as a guide for placement, sew Head to Body.

ARM (Make 2)

Rnd 1 (Right side)**:** With larger size hook and Pink, make an adjustable loop to form a ring; work 6 sc in ring; do **not** join, place marker to indicate beginning of rnd.

Note: Mark Rnd 1 as **right** side.

Rnd 2: 2 Sc in each sc around: 12 sc.

Rnds 3-7: Sc in each sc around.

Rnd 8: (Sc2tog, sc in next 2 sc) around: 9 sc.

Rnds 9-12: Sc in each sc around.

Slip st in next sc, finish off leaving a long end for sewing.

Stuff Arm lightly with polyester fiberfill.

Flatten Arms; using photo on page 20 as a guide for placement, sew Arms to sides of Body using long ends.

EYEBALL (Make 2)

Rnd 1 (Right side)**:** With smaller size hook and Brown, make an adjustable loop to form a ring; work 6 sc in ring; do **not** join, place marker to indicate beginning of rnd.

Rnd 2: 2 Sc in each sc around, changing to White in last sc ***(Fig. 4, page 30)***; cut Brown: 12 sc.

Rnd 3: (2 Sc in next sc, sc in next sc) around: 18 sc.

Rnd 4: (2 Sc in next sc, sc in next 2 sc) around: 24 sc.

Rnds 5-7: Sc in each sc around.

Rnd 8: (Sc2tog, sc in next 2 sc) around: 18 sc.

Stuff Eyeball firmly with polyester fiberfill.

Rnd 9: (Sc2tog, sc in next sc) around: 12 sc.

Rnd 10: Sc2tog around; slip st in next sc, finish off leaving a long end for sewing and to work Stalk: 6 sc.

Thread yarn needle with long end. Weave needle through sts on Rnd 10 and pull **tightly** to close hole and secure end; do **not** cut yarn.

Stalk: With same yarn, insert hook in center back of Eyeball, YO and pull up a loop, ch 4; finish off leaving a long end for sewing.

Using photo as a guide for placement and long ends, sew Stalks to center of Rnd 1 on Head.

EAR (Make 2)

Row 1: With larger size hook and Pink, make an adjustable loop to form a ring; ch 2 **(does not count as a st)**, work 12 hdc in ring; do **not** join.

Row 2 (Right side)**:** Ch 2, turn; 2 hdc in first hdc, hdc in next hdc, (2 hdc in next hdc, hdc in next hdc) across; finish off leaving a long end for sewing: 18 hdc.

Note: Mark Row 2 as **right** side.

Using photo on page 20 as a guide for placement and long ends, sew Ears to Head.

MOUTH

Using photo on page 20 as a guide for placement and outline stitch ***(Figs. 7a & b, page 30)***, add Red mouth to Head.

Minty
Hottie

MINTY

EASY

Finished Size:
Approximately 9" (23 cm) tall

SHOPPING LIST

Yarn (Medium Weight) MEDIUM 4
[7 ounces 364 yards
(198 grams, 333 meters) per skein]:

- ☐ Mint - 1 skein
- ☐ White - 30 yards (27.5 meters)
- ☐ Red - small amount

Crochet Hooks

- ☐ Size E (3.5 mm) **and**
- ☐ Size G (4 mm)

Additional Supplies

- ☐ Yarn needle
- ☐ Polyester fiberfill

GAUGE INFORMATION

Gauge is not of great importance as long as your crochet fabric is dense *(see Gauge, page 29)*.

STITCH GUIDE

SINGLE CROCHET 2 TOGETHER *(abbreviated sc2tog)*
Pull up a loop in each of next 2 sc, YO and draw through all 3 loops on hook **(counts as one sc)**.

SINGLE CROCHET 3 TOGETHER *(abbreviated sc3tog)*
Pull up a loop in each of next 3 sc, YO and draw through all 4 loops on hook **(counts as one sc)**.

BODY

Rnd 1 (Right side)**:** With larger size hook and Mint, make an adjustable loop to form a ring ***(Figs. 1a-d, page 30)***; work 6 sc in ring; do **not** join, place marker to indicate beginning of rnd ***(see Markers, page 29)***.

Rnd 2: 2 Sc in each sc around: 12 sc.

Rnd 3: Sc in each sc around.

Rnd 4: 2 Sc in each sc around: 24 sc.

Rnd 5: (Sc in next sc, 2 sc in next sc) around: 36 sc.

Rnds 6-17: Sc in each sc around; do **not** finish off.

FIRST LEG

Rnd 1: Sc in next 18 sc, leave remaining sc unworked; do **not** join, place marker to indicate beginning of rnd: 18 sc.

Rnd 2: Sc in each sc around.

Rnd 3: Sc in next 3 sc, 2 hdc in each of next 3 sc (toes), sc in each sc around; slip st in next sc, finish off: 21 sts.

SECOND LEG

Rnd 1: With **right** side facing, larger size hook, and leaving a long end for sewing, join Mint with sc in first unworked sc on Rnd 17 of Body ***(see Joining With Sc, page 29)***; sc in each sc around; do **not** join, place marker to indicate beginning of rnd: 18 sc.

Rnd 2: Sc in each sc around.

Rnd 3: Sc in next 12 sc, 2 hdc in each of next 3 sc (toes), sc in next 3 sc; slip st in next sc, finish off : 21 sts.

Thread yarn needle with long end and sew opening between Legs closed.

Stuff Body and Legs firmly with polyester fiberfill.

SOLE (Make 2)

Rnd 1 (Right side)**:** With larger size hook and Mint, make an adjustable loop to form a ring; ch 2 **(does not count as a st)**, work 12 hdc in ring; do **not** join, place marker to indicate beginning of rnd: 12 hdc.

Note: Loop a short piece of yarn around any stitch to mark Rnd 1 as **right** side.

Rnd 2: 2 Hdc in each hdc around; slip st in next hdc, finish off leaving a long end for sewing: 24 hdc.

With long ends, sew one Sole to bottom of each Leg.

HEAD

Rnd 1 (Right side)**:** With larger size hook and Mint, make an adjustable loop to form a ring; work 6 sc in ring; do **not** join, place marker to indicate beginning of rnd.

Rnd 2: 2 Sc in each sc around: 12 sc.

Rnd 3: (2 Sc in next sc, sc in next sc) around: 18 sc.

Rnd 4: (2 Sc in next sc, sc in next 2 sc) around: 24 sc.

Rnd 5: (2 Sc in next sc, sc in next 3 sc) around: 30 sc.

Rnd 6: (2 Sc in next sc, sc in next 4 sc) around: 36 sc.

Rnds 7-11: Sc in each sc around.

Rnd 12: (Sc2tog, sc in next 4 sc) around: 30 sc.

Rnd 13: (Sc2tog, sc in next 3 sc) around: 24 sc.

Rnd 14: (Sc2tog, sc in next 2 sc) around: 18 sc.

Stuff Head firmly with polyester fiberfill.

Rnd 15: (Sc2tog, sc in next sc) around: 12 sc.

Rnd 16: Sc2tog around; slip st in next sc, finish off leaving a long end for sewing: 6 sc.

Thread yarn needle with long end. Weave needle through sts on Rnd 16 ***(Fig. 5, page 30)*** and pull **tightly** to close hole and secure end; do **not** cut yarn.

With same yarn and using photo on page 24 as a guide for placement, sew Head to Body.

ARM (Make 2)

Rnd 1 (Right side)**:** With larger size hook and Mint, make an adjustable loop to form a ring; work 6 sc in ring; do **not** join, place marker to indicate beginning of rnd.

Note: Mark Rnd 1 as **right** side.

Rnd 2: 2 Sc in each sc around: 12 sc.

Rnds 3-7: Sc in each sc around.

Rnd 8: (Sc2tog, sc in next 2 sc) around: 9 sc.

Rnds 9-12: Sc in each sc around.

Slip st in next sc, finish off leaving a long end for sewing.

Stuff Arm lightly with polyester fiberfill.

Flatten Arms; using photo on page 24 as a guide for placement, sew Arms to sides of Body using long ends.

EYEBALL (Make 2)

Rnd 1 (Right side)**:** With smaller size hook and Mint, make an adjustable loop to form a ring; work 6 sc in ring; do **not** join, place marker to indicate beginning of rnd.

Rnd 2: 2 Sc in each sc around, changing to White in last sc ***(Fig. 4, page 30)***; cut Mint: 12 sc.

Rnd 3: (2 Sc in next sc, sc in next sc) around: 18 sc.

Rnd 4: (2 Sc in next sc, sc in next 2 sc) around: 24 sc.

Rnds 5-7: Sc in each sc around.

Rnd 8: (Sc2tog, sc in next 2 sc) around: 18 sc.

Stuff Eye firmly with polyester fiberfill.

Rnd 9: (Sc2tog, sc in next sc) around: 12 sc.

Rnd 10: Sc2tog around; slip st in next sc, finish off leaving a long end for sewing: 6 sc.

Thread yarn needle with long end. Weave needle through sts on Rnd 10 and pull **tightly** to close hole and secure end.

Using photo on page 24 as a guide for placement and White, sew Eyeballs to Head.

EAR (Make 2)

With smaller size hook, Mint, and leaving a long end for sewing, ch 10.

Row 1 (Right side)**:** Sc in second ch from hook and in each ch across: 9 sc.

Note: Mark Row 1 as **right** side.

Row 2: Ch 1, turn; sc in each sc across.

Rows 3 and 4: Ch 1, turn; beginning in first sc, sc2tog, sc in each sc across to last 2 sc, sc2tog: 5 sc.

Row 5: Ch 1, turn; beginning in first sc, sc2tog, sc in next sc, sc2tog: 3 sc.

Row 6: Ch 1, turn; sc3tog; finish off.

Thread yarn needle with long end. Cupping Row 1 of Ear, sew to Head using photo on page 24 as a guide for placement.

MOUTH

Using photo on page 24 as a guide for placement and outline stitch ***(Figs. 7a & b, page 30)***, add Red mouth to Head.

HOTTIE

●●○○ EASY

Finished Size:
Approximately 9" (23 cm) tall

SHOPPING LIST

Yarn (Medium Weight) MEDIUM 4
[7 ounces 364 yards
(198 grams, 333 meters) per skein]:
- ☐ Red - 1 skein
- ☐ White - 20 yards (18.5 meters)
- ☐ Brown - small amount
- ☐ Tan - small amount

Crochet Hooks
- ☐ Size E (3.5 mm) **and**
- ☐ Size G (4 mm)

Additional Supplies
- ☐ Yarn needle
- ☐ Polyester fiberfill

GAUGE INFORMATION

Gauge is not of great importance as long as your crochet fabric is dense *(see Gauge, page 29)*.

STITCH GUIDE

SINGLE CROCHET 2 TOGETHER *(abbreviated sc2tog)*
Pull up a loop in each of next 2 sc, YO and draw through all 3 loops on hook **(counts as one sc)**.

BODY

Rnd 1 (Right side)**:** With larger size hook and Red, make an adjustable loop to form a ring ***(Figs. 1a-d, page 30)***; work 6 sc in ring; do **not** join, place marker to indicate beginning of rnd ***(see Markers, page 29)***.

Rnd 2: 2 Sc in each sc around: 12 sc.

Rnd 3: Sc in each sc around.

Rnd 4: 2 Sc in each sc around: 24 sc.

Rnd 5: (Sc in next sc, 2 sc in next sc) around: 36 sc.

Rnds 6-17: Sc in each sc around; do **not** finish off.

FIRST LEG

Rnd 1: Sc in next 18 sc, leave remaining sc unworked; do **not** join, place marker to indicate beginning of rnd: 18 sc.

Rnd 2: Sc in each sc around.

Rnd 3: Sc in next 3 sc, 2 hdc in each of next 3 sc (toes), sc in each sc around; slip st in next sc, finish off: 21 sts.

SECOND LEG

Rnd 1: With **right** side facing, larger size hook, and leaving a long end for sewing, join Red with sc in first unworked sc on Rnd 17 of Body ***(see Joining With Sc, page 29)***; sc in each sc around; do **not** join, place marker to indicate beginning of rnd: 18 sc.

Rnd 2: Sc in each sc around.

Rnd 3: Sc in next 12 sc, 2 hdc in each of next 3 sc (toes), sc in next 3 sc; slip st in next sc, finish off: 21 sts.

Thread yarn needle with long end and sew opening between Legs closed.

Stuff Body and Legs firmly with polyester fiberfill.

SOLE (Make 2)

Rnd 1 (Right side)**:** With larger size hook and Red, make an adjustable loop to form a ring; ch 2 **(does not count as a st)**, work 12 hdc in ring; do **not** join, place marker to indicate beginning of rnd: 12 hdc.

Note: Loop a short piece of yarn around any stitch to mark Rnd 1 as **right** side.

Rnd 2: 2 Hdc in each hdc around; slip st in next hdc, finish off leaving a long end for sewing: 24 hdc.

With long ends, sew one Sole to bottom of each Leg.

HEAD

Rnd 1 (Right side)**:** With larger size hook and Red, make an adjustable loop to form a ring; work 6 sc in ring; do **not** join, place marker to indicate beginning of rnd.

Rnd 2: 2 Sc in each sc around: 12 sc.

Rnd 3: (2 Sc in next sc, sc in next sc) around: 18 sc.

Rnd 4: (2 Sc in next sc, sc in next 2 sc) around: 24 sc.

Rnd 5: (2 Sc in next sc, sc in next 3 sc) around: 30 sc.

Rnd 6: (2 Sc in next sc, sc in next 4 sc) around: 36 sc.

Rnds 7-11: Sc in each sc around.

Rnd 12: (Sc2tog, sc in next 4 sc) around: 30 sc.

Rnd 13: (Sc2tog, sc in next 3 sc) around: 24 sc.

Rnd 14: (Sc2tog, sc in next 2 sc) around: 18 sc.

Stuff Head firmly with polyester fiberfill.

Rnd 15: (Sc2tog, sc in next sc) around: 12 sc.

Rnd 16: Sc2tog around; slip st in next sc, finish off leaving a long end for sewing: 6 sc.

Thread yarn needle with long end. Weave needle through sts on Rnd 16 ***(Fig. 5, page 30)*** and pull **tightly** to close hole and secure end; do **not** cut yarn.

With same yarn and using photo on page 24 as a guide for placement, sew Head to Body.

ARM (Make 4)

Rnd 1 (Right side)**:** With larger size hook and Red, make an adjustable loop to form a ring; work 6 sc in ring; do **not** join, place marker to indicate beginning of rnd.

Note: Mark Rnd 1 as **right** side.

Rnd 2: 2 Sc in each sc around: 12 sc.

Rnds 3-7: Sc in each sc around.

Rnd 8: (Sc2tog, sc in next 2 sc) around: 9 sc.

Rnds 9-12: Sc in each sc around.

Slip st in next sc, finish off leaving a long end for sewing.

Stuff Arm lightly with polyester fiberfill.

Flatten Arms; using photo on page 24 as a guide for placement, sew 2 Arms to each side of Body using long ends.

EYEBALL (Make 3)

Rnd 1 (Right side)**:** With smaller size hook and Brown, make an adjustable loop to form a ring; work 6 sc in ring; do **not** join, place marker to indicate beginning of rnd.

Rnd 2: 2 Sc in each sc around, changing to White in last sc ***(Fig. 4, page 30)***; cut Brown: 12 sc.

Rnd 3: Sc in each sc around.

Rnd 4: (2 Sc in next sc, sc in next sc) around: 18 sc.

Rnd 5: Sc in each sc around.

Stuff Eye firmly with polyester fiberfill.

Rnd 6: (Sc2tog, sc in next sc) around: 12 sc.

Rnd 7: Sc2tog around; slip st in next sc, finish off leaving a long end for sewing: 6 sc.

Thread yarn needle with long end. Weave needle through sts on Rnd 7 and pull **tightly** to close hole and secure end.

Using photo on page 24 as a guide for placement and White, sew Eyeballs to Head.

MOUTH

Using photo on page 24 as a guide for placement and outline stitch ***(Figs. 7a & b, page 30)***, add Tan mouth to Head.

GENERAL INSTRUCTIONS

ABBREVIATIONS

ch(s)	chain(s)
cm	centimeters
hdc	half double crochet(s)
mm	millimeters
Rnd(s)	Round(s)
sc	single crochet(s)
sc2tog	single crochet 2 together
sc3tog	single crochet 3 together
st(s)	stitch(es)
YO	yarn over

SYMBOLS & TERMS

( ) or **[ ]** — work enclosed instructions **as many** times as specified by the number immediately following **or** contains explanatory remarks.

colon (:) — the number(s) given after a colon at the end of a row or round denote(s) the number of stitches you should have on that row or round.

GAUGE

Gauge is not of great importance; your project may be a little larger or smaller without changing the overall effect. It is best to use a small hook and tight single crochet stitches. The holes between the stitches need to be very small, making your crochet fabric dense. The stuffing should not stretch the fabric or show through the stitches. Use the size hook needed to achieve a tight gauge.

CROCHET TERMINOLOGY		
UNITED STATES		INTERNATIONAL
slip stitch (slip st)	=	single crochet (sc)
single crochet (sc)	=	double crochet (dc)
half double crochet (hdc)	=	half treble crochet (htr)
double crochet (dc)	=	treble crochet (tr)
treble crochet (tr)	=	double treble crochet (dtr)
double treble crochet (dtr)	=	triple treble crochet (ttr)
triple treble crochet (tr tr)	=	quadruple treble crochet (qtr)
skip	=	miss

Yarn Weight Symbol & Names	LACE 0	SUPER FINE 1	FINE 2	LIGHT 3	MEDIUM 4	BULKY 5	SUPER BULKY 6	JUMBO 7
Type of Yarns in Category	Fingering, size 10 crochet thread	Sock, Fingering, Baby	Sport, Baby	DK, Light Worsted	Worsted, Afghan, Aran	Chunky, Craft, Rug	Super Bulky, Roving	Jumbo, Roving
Crochet Gauge* Ranges in Single Crochet to 4" (10 cm)	32-42 sts**	21-32 sts	16-20 sts	12-17 sts	11-14 sts	8-11 sts	6-9 sts	5 sts and fewer
Advised Hook Size Range	Steel*** 6 to 8, Regular hook B-1	B-1 to E-4	E-4 to 7	7 to I-9	I-9 to K-10½	K-10½ to M/N-13	M/N-13 to Q	Q and larger

*GUIDELINES ONLY: The chart above reflects the most commonly used gauges and hook sizes for specific yarn categories.

MARKERS

Markers are used to help distinguish the beginning of each round being worked. Place a 2" (5 cm) scrap piece of yarn before the first stitch of each round, moving the marker after each round is complete.

JOINING WITH SC

When instructed to join with sc, begin with a slip knot on hook. Insert hook in stitch indicated, YO and pull up a loop, YO and draw through both loops on hook.

CROCHET HOOKS																	
U.S.	B-1	C-2	D-3	E-4	F-5	G-6	7	H-8	I-9	J-10	K-10½	L-11	M/N-13	N/P-15	P/Q	Q	S
Metric - mm	2.25	2.75	3.25	3.5	3.75	4	4.5	5	5.5	6	6.5	8	9	10	15	16	19

●○○○ **BEGINNER**	Projects for first-time crocheters using basic stitches. Minimal shaping.
●●○○ **EASY**	Projects using yarn with basic stitches, repetitive stitch patterns, simple color changes, and simple shaping and finishing.
●●●○ **INTERMEDIATE**	Projects using a variety of techniques, such as basic lace patterns or color patterns, mid-level shaping and finishing.
●●●● **EXPERIENCED**	Projects with intricate stitch patterns, techniques and dimension, such as non-repeating patterns, multi-color techniques, fine threads, small hooks, detailed shaping and refined finishing.

ADJUSTABLE LOOP

Wind the yarn around two fingers to form a ring *(Fig. 1a)*, slide the yarn off your fingers and grasp the strands at the top to the ring *(Fig. 1b)*. Insert the hook from **front** to **back** into the ring, pull up a loop, YO and draw through the loop on hook to lock the ring *(Fig. 1c)*.

Working around **both** strands, work stitches in the ring as specified, then pull the yarn end to close *(Fig. 1d)*.

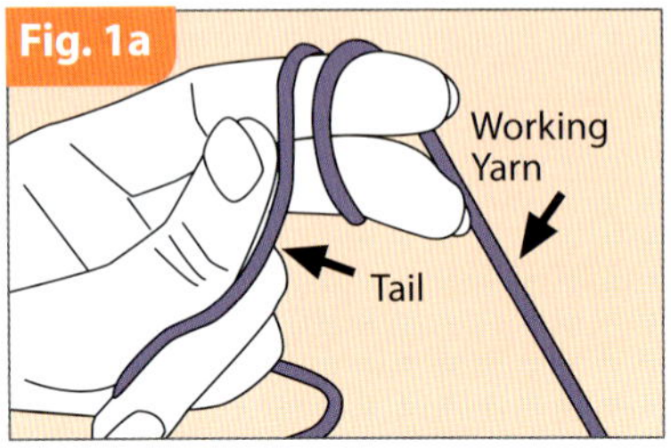

Fig. 1a

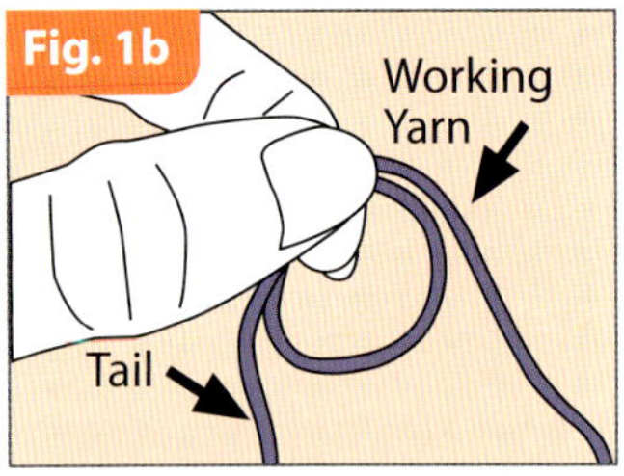

Fig. 1b

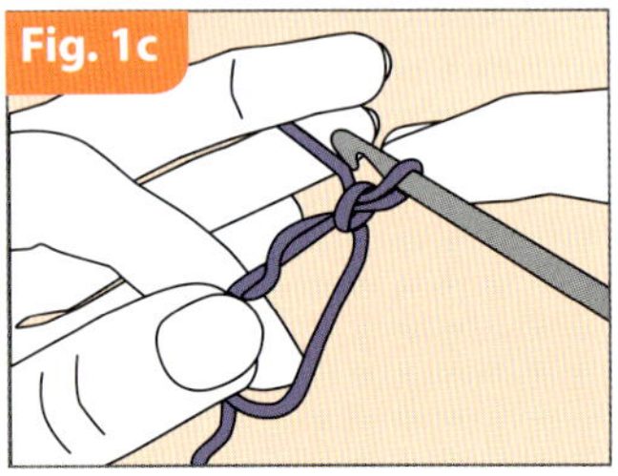
Fig. 1c

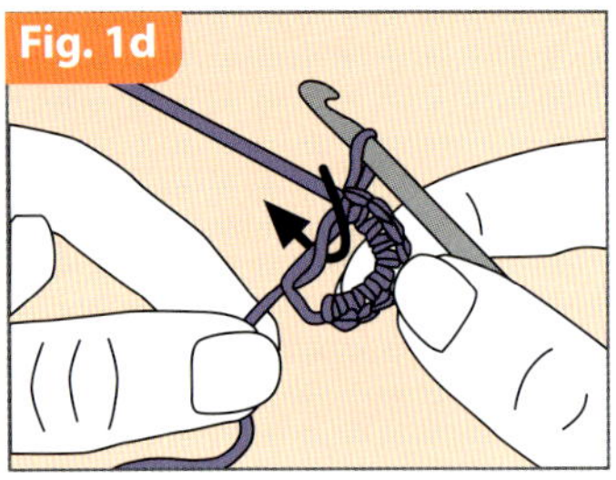
Fig. 1d

BACK RIDGE OF A CHAIN

Work only in loops indicated by arrows *(Fig. 2)*.

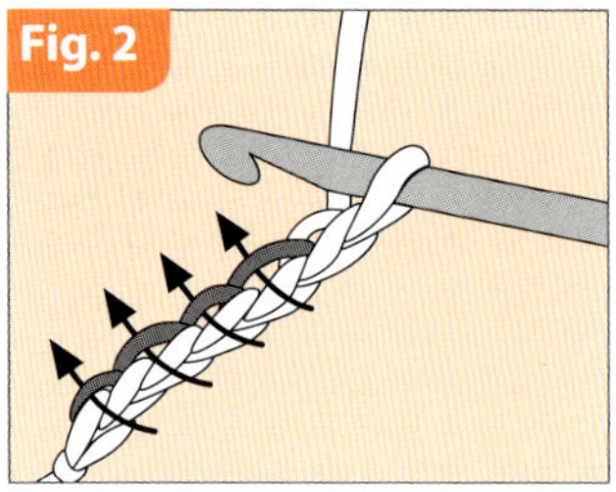
Fig. 2

BACK LOOPS ONLY

Work only in loop(s) indicated by arrow *(Fig. 3)*.

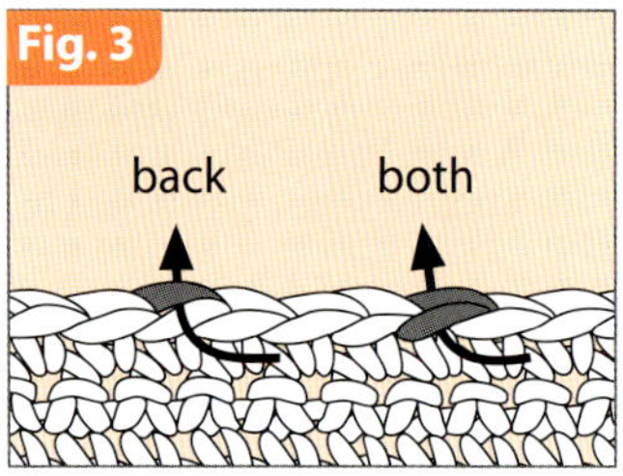

Fig. 3

CHANGING COLORS

Work the last stitch to within one step of completion, hook new yarn *(Fig. 4)* and draw though loops on hook.

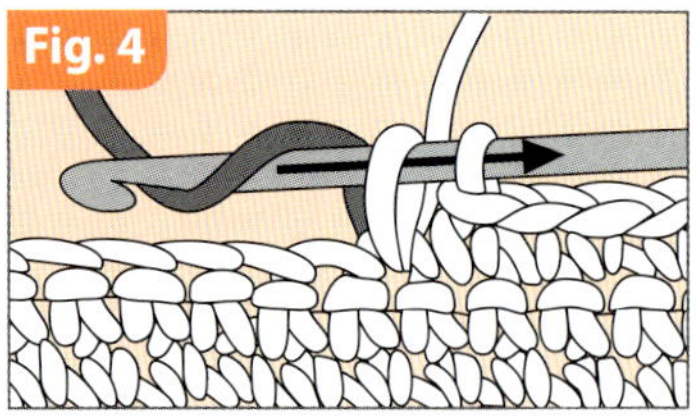
Fig. 4

WEAVE THRU STITCHES

Weave yarn end through the stitches *(Fig. 5)* and gather to close.

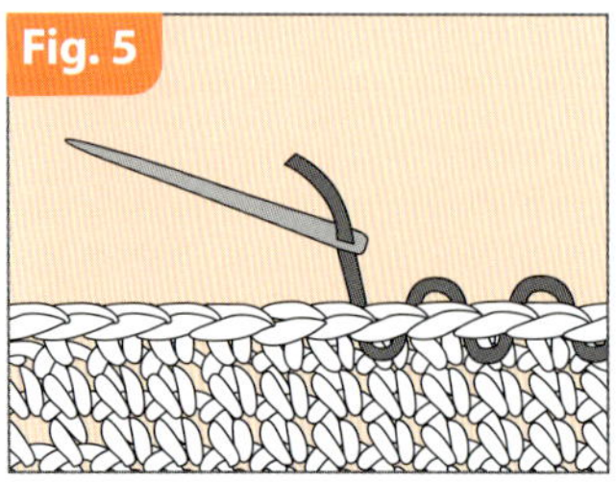
Fig. 5

WHIPSTITCH

With **wrong** side together, sew through both pieces once to secure the beginning of the seam, leaving an ample yarn end to weave in later. Insert the needle from **back** to **front** through **both** loops on **both** pieces *(Fig. 6)*. Bring the needle around and insert it from **back** to **front** through the next loops of both pieces. Continue in this manner across to corner, keeping the sewing yarn fairly loose.

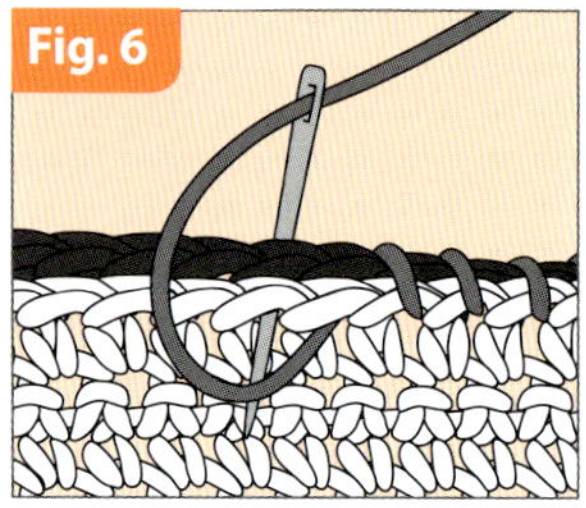
Fig. 6

OUTLINE STITCH

Bring needle up at 1, leaving an end to be woven in later. Holding yarn **above** with thumb, insert needle down at 2 and up again at 3 (halfway between 1 and 2) *(Fig. 7a)*; pull through. Insert needle down at 4 and up again at 2, making sure yarn is **above** needle *(Fig. 7b)*; pull through.

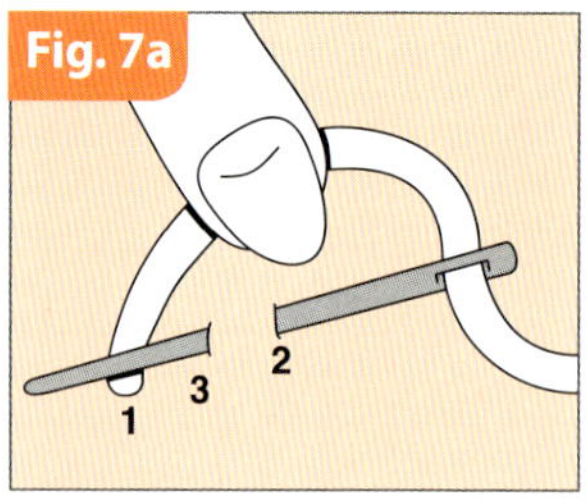

Fig. 7a

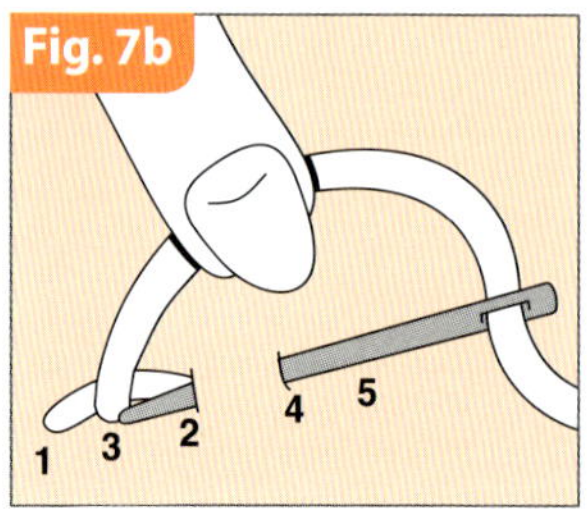

Fig. 7b

YARN INFORMATION

The Monsters in this book were made using Red Heart® Super Saver®, a Medium Weight yarn. Any brand of medium weight yarn may be used. It is best to refer to the yardage/meters when determining how many balls or skeins to purchase. Remember, to arrive at the finished size, it is the GAUGE/TENSION that is important, not the brand of yarn.

For your convenience, listed below are the colors used to create our photography models. Because yarn manufacturers make frequent changes in their product lines, you may sometimes find it necessary to use a substitute yarn or to search for the discontinued product at alternate suppliers (locally or online).

SUNNY
Yellow - #324 Bright Yellow
White - #311 White
Brown - #365 Coffee
Pink - #718 Shocking Pink
Grey - #400 Grey Heather

POM-POM
Blue - #506 Pool
Yellow - #324 Bright Yellow
White - #311 White
Brown - #365 Coffee
Red - #390 Hot Red

MOHAWK
Green - #3620 Glowworm
White - #311 White
Brown - #365 Coffee
Red - #319 Cherry Red

FLAME
Orange - #3251 Flame
White - #311 White
Brown - #365 Coffee
Red - #319 Cherry Red

FLOPPY
Blue - #512 Turqua
White - #311 White
Red - #390 Hot Red

SHOCKSTER
Pink - #718 Shocking Pink
White - #311 White
Brown - #365 Coffee
Red - #390 Hot Red

SINGLETON
Purple - #776 Dark Orchid
White - #311 White
Blue - #506 Pool
Red - #319 Cherry Red
Grey - #400 Grey Heather

PINKY
Pink - #722 Pretty 'n Pink
White - #311 White
Brown - #365 Coffee
Red - #390 Hot Red

MINTY
Green - #520 Minty
White - #311 White
Red - #390 Hot Red

HOTTIE
Red - #390 Hot Red
Brown - #365 Coffee
White - #311 White
Tan - #360 Café Latte

Meet the Designer:

Yolanda Soto-Lopez

Yolanda Soto-Lopez is an avid sewist, knit and crochet designer, and craft enthusiast. She enjoys sharing her creations with others and has made it her mission to spread the love of creativity. Most of her crochet, knitting, and sewing creations are items that have been requested by her grandchildren.

She spent her early childhood in Chihuahua, Mexico, where she learned to crochet and knit from her aunts Maria Gonzales and Guadalupe Alvarez. She learned to sew from her mother. Some of her fondest childhood memories involved sewing together with her mother and crafting with other members of her family. "It was always a time to share love, good food, and lots of fun," she says.

Her motto is "If you aren't having fun, it's not worth doing." Yolanda's creations may be found on her YouTube channel (the "All Crafts Channel") and on her blog at allcraftschannel.com. Other Leisure Arts books featuring her designs include *Animal Lovies to Knit* (#6645) and *Animal Lovies to Crochet* (#6373).

Yolanda lives in Southern California with her husband and two dogs.

We have made every effort to ensure that these instructions are accurate and complete. We cannot, however, be responsible for human error, typographical mistakes, or variations in individual work.

Production Team: Instructional/Technical Writer - Lois J. Long; Editorial Writer - Susan Frantz Wiles; Senior Graphic Artist - Lora Puls; Graphic Artists - Kellie McAnulty and Victoria Temple; Photo Stylist - Lori Wenger; and Photographer - Jason Masters.

Made in China